Add and subtract 1 a

24 + 10 = ☐

22 − ☐ = 12

49 − 10 = ☐

38 + 10 = ☐

13 + ☐ = 14

93 − 1 = ☐

51 − ☐ = 41

84 − 10 = ☐

76 − 10 = ☐

85 + ☐ = 95

17 + 10 = ☐

99 − 10 = ☐

38 + 1 = ☐

49 − ☐ = 48

Write the missing number in the box for each question.

 ACTION Use Spider on a 100-square to help you.

THINK Which digit changes when you add or subtract 1? Which digit changes when you add or subtract 10?

3

Adding and subtracting with cartoons

Not all of these questions match a cartoon!

43 + 1 = ☐

56 + 10 = ☐

56 − 10 = ☐

31 − 10 = ☐

72 − 10 = ☐

22 − 1 = ☐

56p

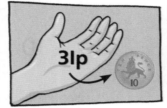
94p

31p

67p

72p

45p

23p

88p

92 − 1 = ☐

45 + 10 = ☐

88 − 10 = ☐

88 − 1 = ☐

94 − 1 = ☐

67 + 1 = ☐

23 + 1 = ☐

Match the addition or subtraction to the correct cartoon. Complete the addition or subtraction for each match.

ACTION Use Spider on a 100-square to help you.

THINK Choose a number between 50 and 90. Add 11. What happens to the digits?

4

abacus

Year 1
Workbook 3

PEARSON

1 more, 1 less; 10 more, 10 less

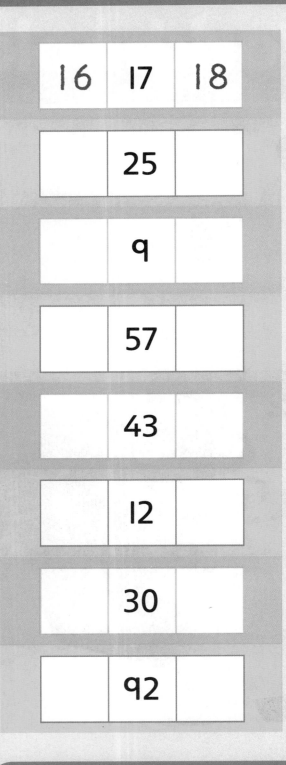

16	17	18

	25	

	9	

	57	

	43	

	12	

	30	

	92	

50	60	70

	21	

	15	

	30	

	66	

	53	

	82	

	29	

Write 1 more and 1 less next to each number in the first column. Write 10 more and 10 less next to each number in the second column.

 ACTION Use a 100-square to help you.

 THINK Choose a number from the first column and a number from the second column. How many numbers are between them?

Finding totals of 10p and 1p stacks

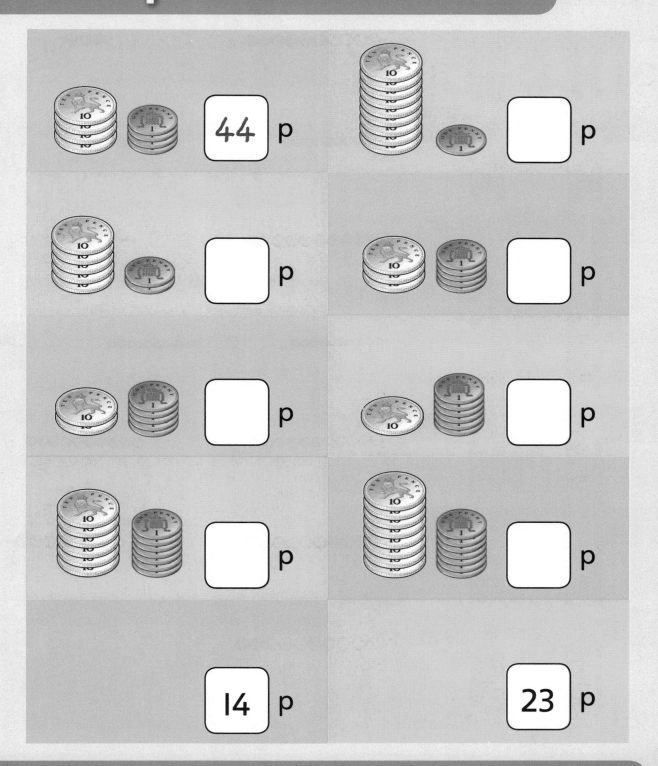

Write the total beside each amount. Draw coins to match the last two totals.

THINK You have 7 coins. They make 34p. What coins are they?

10s and 1s in 2-digit numbers

23 = 20 + 3

☐ = ☐ + ☐

☐ = ☐ + ☐

☐ = ☐ + ☐

☐ = ☐ + ☐

☐ = ☐ + ☐

☐ = ☐ + ☐

How many beads are there? Fill in the tag and complete the addition to find out.

 ACTION Use a bead string to help you.

 THINK Make a 2-digit number on a bead string for your partner. Can your partner tell you the number and how many 10s and 1s it contains?

Number bonds

4p + 3p = ⬜ p

⬜ p + ⬜ p = ⬜ p

14p + 5p = ⬜ p

⬜ p + ⬜ p = ⬜ p

1p + 5p = ⬜ p

11p + 5p = ⬜ p

21p + 5p = ⬜ p

31p + 5p = ⬜ p

41p + 5p = ⬜ p

51p + 5p = ⬜ p

5p + 4p = ⬜ p

15p + 4p = ⬜ p

25p + 4p = ⬜ p

35p + 4p = ⬜ p

45p + 4p = ⬜ p

55p + 4p = ⬜ p

Complete all the additions on this page using your number bonds.

 ACTION Use real coins and bond posters to help you.

 THINK Use 4 + 2 = 6 to make the biggest similar addition that you can, for example 34 + 2 = 36.

Bonds to 6, 7, 8 and 9

☐ p – 2p = ☐ p   ☐ p – 3p = ☐ p

18p – 2p = ☐ p   27p – 4p = ☐ p

36p – 3p = ☐ p   19p – 5p = ☐ p

8p – 5p = ☐ p   7p – 3p = ☐ p

18p – 5p = ☐ p   17p – 3p = ☐ p

28p – 5p = ☐ p   27p – 3p = ☐ p

38p – 5p = ☐ p   37p – 3p = ☐ p

48p – 5p = ☐ p   47p – 3p = ☐ p

58p – 5p = ☐ p   57p – 3p = ☐ p

Use the pictures to answer the first two questions. Then fill in the missing numbers.

 ACTION Use real coins and bond posters to help you.

 **THINK** 97 – 2 = 95
87 – 2 = 85

Keep going. Write as many subtractions as you can like this.

Adding 1-digit numbers

5	⑥	7	8	9	10	11

						12

19	18	17	16	15	14	13

6 + 4 = ☐

6	7	⑧	9	10	11	12

						13

						14

8 + 4 = ☐

⑧	9	10	11	12	13	14

						15

						16

8 + 7 = ☐

5	6	⑦	8	9	10	11

						12

				15	14	13

7 + 6 = ☐

8	⑨	10	11	12	13	14

						15

						16

9 + 3 = ☐

4	5	6	7	8	⑨	10

						11

					13	12

9 + 2 = ☐

3	4	5	6	⑦	8	9

						10

		15	14	13	12	11

7 + 5 = ☐

5	6	7	⑧	9	10	11

						12

	17	16	15	14	13

8 + 5 = ☐

Use the number tracks to complete the additions.

 ACTION Use a counter. Put it on the first number and count on to the second number. Or, use a bead string.

 THINK Choose an addition. Start with the answer. Write a subtraction to match.

Additions totalling more than 10

9 + 5 = ☐   8 + 3 = ☐

7 + 5 = ☐   6 + 7 = ☐

☐ + ☐ = ☐   ☐ + ☐ = ☐

☐ + ☐ = ☐   ☐ + ☐ = ☐

Complete the additions. Then choose two cars and write an addition with an answer bigger than 10. Do this four times.

 ACTION Use a bonds poster to help you choose numbers which add to more than 10. Use a number track or a bead string to help you find the totals.

 THINK Choose three cars. What is the largest total you can make? What is the smallest?

Additions

Just know

7 + 3 = ☐

4 + 4 = ☐

10 + 7 = ☐

4 + 6 = ☐

30 + 6 = ☐

15 + 5 = ☐

Work it out

14 + 5 = ☐

24 + 7 = ☐

19 + 6 = ☐

43 + 4 = ☐

35 + 3 = ☐

52 + 6 = ☐

Complete the easy additions in the left-hand column. Then complete the ones you have to work out in the right-hand column.

 ACTION Use bonds posters to help you.

 THINK Write a 'just know' and a 'work it out' subtraction and solve them.

11

Adding three small numbers

4 + 7 + 3 = ☐

9 + 7 + 1 = ☐

3 + 5 + 5 = ☐

6 + 6 + 4 = ☐

6 + 8 + 4 = ☐

Look for pairs to 10!

5 + 5   8 + 2

4 + 6   7 + 3

9 + 1

☐ + ☐ + ☐ = ☐

☐ + ☐ + ☐ = ☐

☐ + ☐ + ☐ = ☐

☐ + ☐ + ☐ = ☐

Complete the additions, looking out for bonds to 10.
Next, choose any three balloons and add them together. Do this again three more times.

 ACTION Use bond posters to help you.

 THINK  ☐ + ☐ + ☐ = 21

Write the same number in each box to get the answer 21.

Adding three small numbers

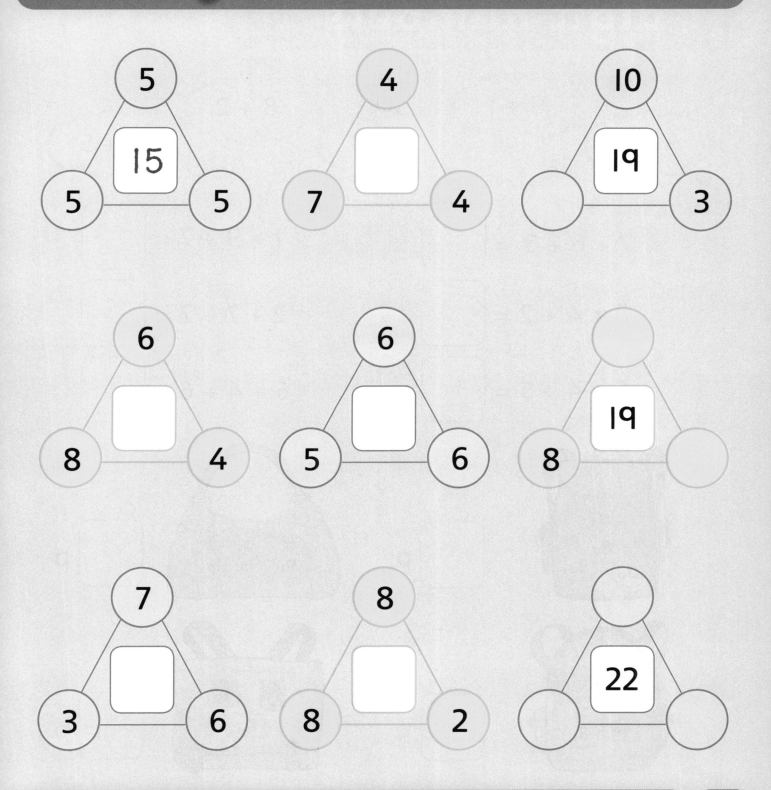

Add the numbers on each triangle. Write the total in the box.
Look at the total in the box. Work out what numbers could be in the circles.

 ACTION Use bond posters and doubles posters to help you.

 THINK Can you make another triangle using three different numbers that has 22 in the middle?

13

Adding three 1-digit numbers

9 + 1

4 + 6

8 + 2

7 + 3

5 + 5

7 + 6 + 3 = ☐

1 + 9 + 7 = ☐

8 + 4 + 2 = ☐

2 + 7 + 2 = ☐

5 + 4 + 5 = ☐

6 + 4 + 6 = ☐

 ☐ p

  ☐ p

 ☐ p

  ☐ p

Look for the cloud pairs as you add the numbers. Then work out how much money is in each bag.

  Use a 1–20 bead string or number track to help you.

THINK ☐ + ☐ + ☐ = 7

Put numbers in the boxes to make this sum work.

Adding three 1-digit numbers

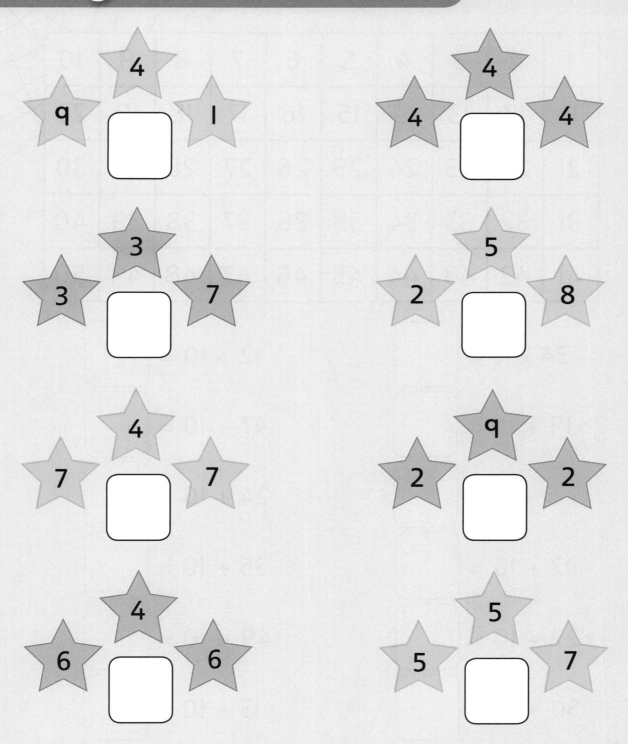

Add up the stars to find the total. Write your answer in the box under the stars.

 Use bead strings and double posters to help you.

 Write an addition of 1-digit numbers where the answer is bigger than 20.

Adding 10 using a number-square

1	2	3	4	5	6	7	8	9	10
11	12	13	14	15	16	17	18	19	20
21	22	23	24	25	26	27	28	29	30
31	32	33	34	35	36	37	38	39	40
41	42	43	44	45	46	47	48	49	50

34 + 10 = ☐   12 + 10 = ☐

19 + 10 = ☐   47 + 10 = ☐

5 + 10 = ☐   24 + 10 = ☐

12 + 10 = ☐   35 + 10 = ☐

22 + 10 = ☐   49 + 10 = ☐

50 + 10 = ☐   13 + 10 = ☐

Complete the '+ 10' additions. Use the number-square to help you.

 ACTION Use 10p and 1p coins to help you make the first number.

 THINK 10 + ☐ = 90. What number goes in the box?

Add and then subtract 10

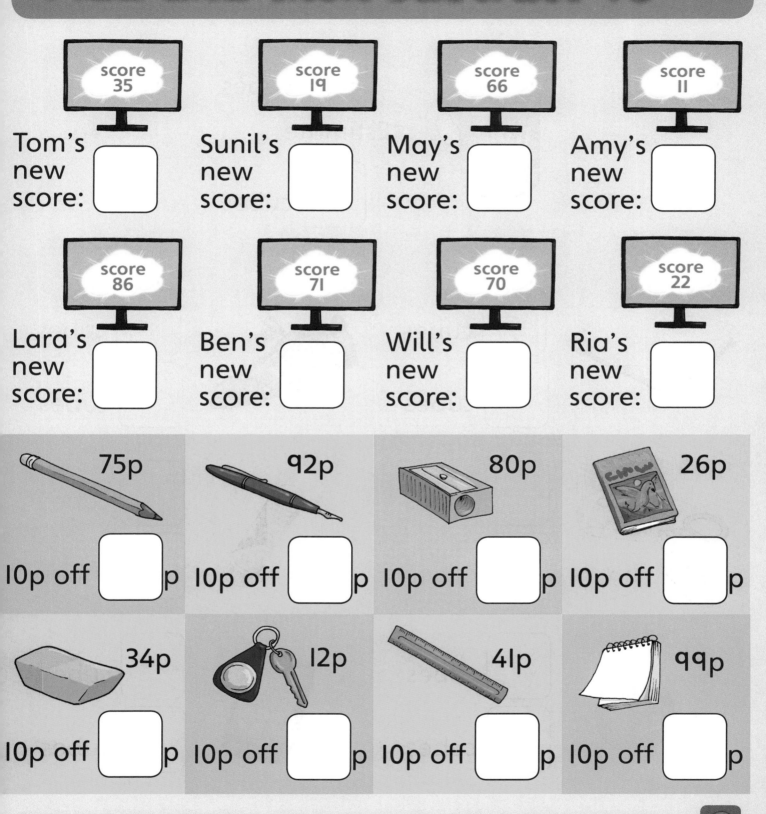

score
35

Tom's
new
score:

score
19

Sunil's
new
score:

score
66

May's
new
score:

score
11

Amy's
new
score:

score
86

Lara's
new
score:

score
71

Ben's
new
score:

score
70

Will's
new
score:

score
22

Ria's
new
score:

75p
10p off [   ]p

92p
10p off [   ]p

80p
10p off [   ]p

26p
10p off [   ]p

34p
10p off [   ]p

12p
10p off [   ]p

41p
10p off [   ]p

99p
10p off [   ]p

Add 10 to each child's score on the screens. Take 10p off each price.

 ACTION   Use a 100-square to help you.

 THINK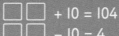
□□ + 10 = 104
□□ − 10 = 4

Write the correct digits in the boxes.

How heavy?

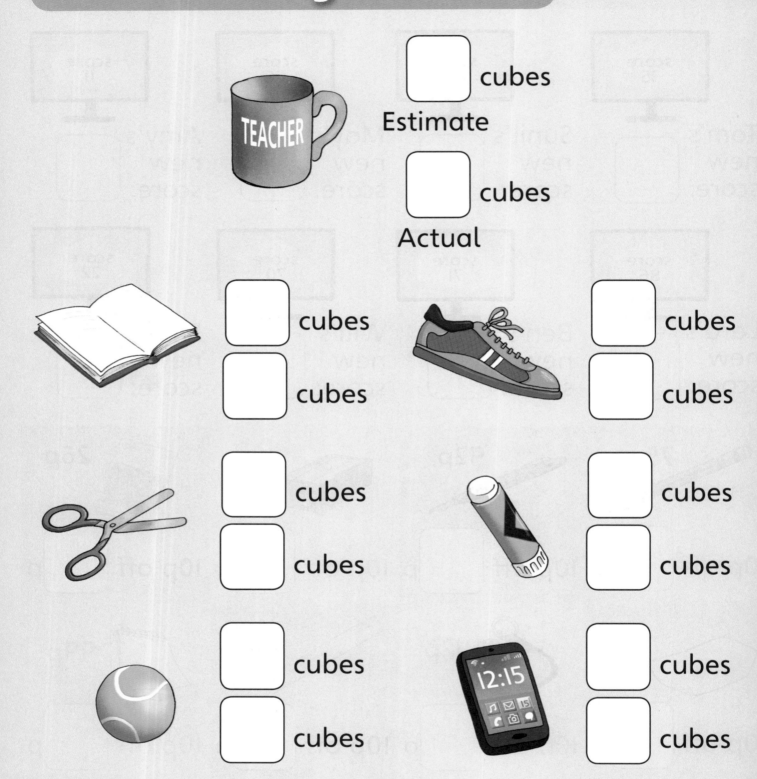

TEACHER

☐ cubes
Estimate

☐ cubes
Actual

☐ cubes
☐ cubes

☐ cubes
☐ cubes

☐ cubes
☐ cubes

☐ cubes
☐ cubes

☐ cubes
☐ cubes

☐ cubes
☐ cubes

Find these objects in the classroom. Estimate how many cubes each object weighs, then use a bucket balance to check.

 Put these objects in order from the lightest to the heaviest, using your hands as a bucket balance.

 Choose one of these objects. Find another object that weighs double the number of cubes.

Heavier and lighter

Find each pair of objects in the classroom. Draw a ring around which object you think is the heavier in each pair. Use the bucket balance to check. Tick the heavier object.

 ACTION Find two objects in the classroom to compare. Which is lighter? Which is heavier?

 THINK Choose a book. Find three objects heavier than the book and three objects lighter than the book.

Capacity

half full

nearly empty

nearly full

nearly full

nearly empty

full

half empty

empty

Colour the drink left in each glass.

 ACTION Arrange three glasses in order: nearly full, half full, empty.

 THINK Fill a bottle with water and draw it. Pour some water out and draw again. Repeat until empty. Label each drawing.

Capacity

Colour in blue any container which could hold more water than a mug. Colour in red any container which holds less water than a mug.

 Use containers and water to help you.

 Draw the objects in order of capacity from smallest to biggest.

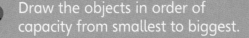

21

Halving numbers of dots up to 12

$\frac{1}{2}$ of 8 is ☐

$\frac{1}{2}$ of 10 is ☐

$\frac{1}{2}$ of 6 is ☐

$\frac{1}{2}$ of 12 is ☐

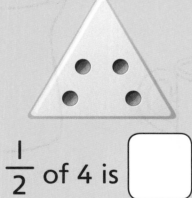

$\frac{1}{2}$ of 4 is ☐

Draw a line through each shape to halve the dots. Then fill in what half of the dots make.

 ACTION Use a tower of interlocking cubes and split them in half to help you.

 THINK Halve the even numbers: 2, 4, 6, 8, … What do you notice about the answers?

Adding coins

Write the amount in each purse.

 ACTION   Use real coins to help you.

 THINK   What different amounts can you make using two pairs of coins, for example 5p + 5p and 2p + 2p?

23

Matching equivalent amounts of money

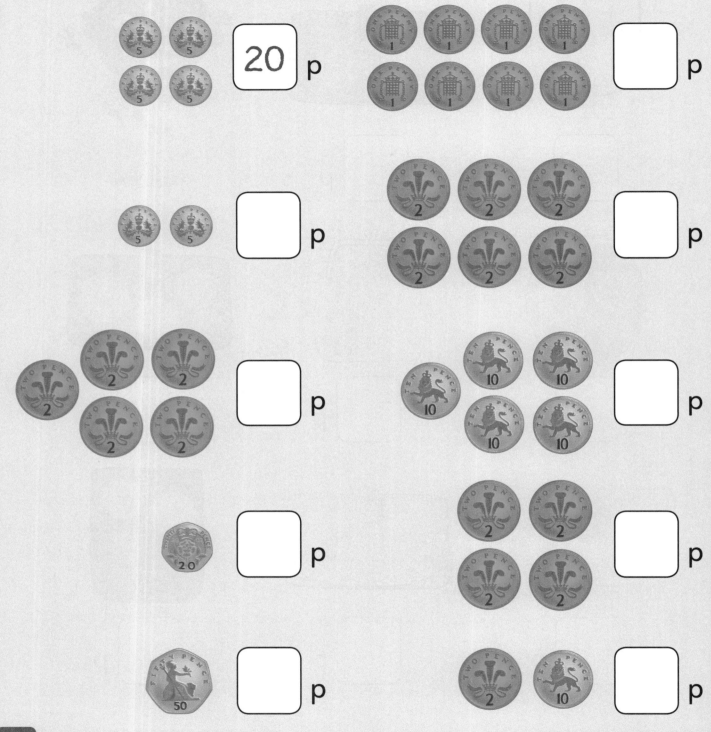

	20 p		p
	p		p
	p		p
	p		p
	p		p

Write the total amount in each box. Draw lines to match equal amounts.

 ACTION Use real coins to help you.

 THINK Make 40p in two different ways. Use only one type of coin each time.

Gaps in a 100-square

1	2	3	4	5	6	7	8	9	10
11	12	13	14	15	16		18	19	20
21	22		24	25	26			29	
31	32			35	36	37	38	39	40
41					46		48	49	50
51	52	53	54	55				59	60
			64		66		68	69	70
			74		76	77	78	79	80
			84					89	90
91	92	93	94		96	97	98	99	100

Fill in the gaps on this 100-square.

 Use a complete 100-square to help you.

 Write the next 10 numbers.

Ordering numbers and finding numbers between

3 14

3 7 8 12 14 ◯ ◯ ◯ ◯ ◯

69 56

45 55

◻ ◯ ◯ ◯ ◻

72 67

◻ ◯ ◯ ◯ ◻

24 17

◻ ◯ ◯ ◯ ◻

31 44

◻ ◯ ◯ ◯ ◻

20 40

◻ ◯ ◯ ◯ ◻

83 54

◻ ◯ ◯ ◯ ◻

Write the two card numbers in order, smallest to largest. Then write any three numbers that come in between.

 ACTION Use a number track to help you.

 THINK Find three pairs of numbers where the middle number is 60.

Ordering 2-digit numbers and writing numbers between

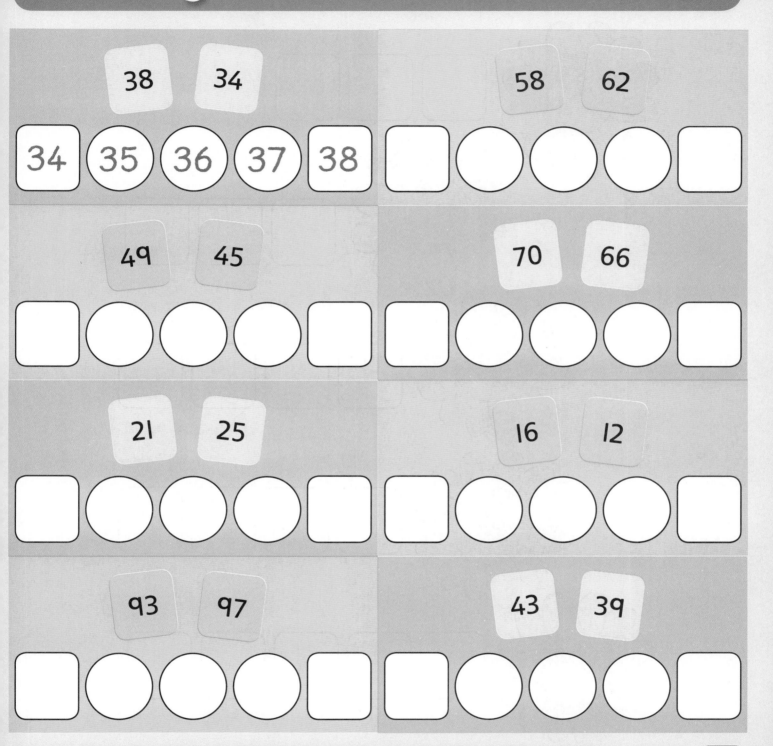

| 38 | 34 | | | | | 58 | 62 |

34 35 36 37 38

| 49 | 45 | | | | | 70 | 66 |

| 21 | 25 | | | | | 16 | 12 |

| 93 | 97 | | | | | 43 | 39 |

Write the smallest number on the left and the biggest on the right. Write the numbers that come between them in the right order.

 ACTION Use a number track to help you.

 THINK Choose a number with next-door digits, for example, 23. Reverse the digits (32). How many numbers are there in between the two numbers? Try another set. What do you notice?

Ordering groups of 2-digit numbers

Write each set of numbers in order, smallest to largest.

 ACTION Use a number track to help you.

 THINK Choose one of the rows. Write a number in between each pair of numbers.

Creating 2-digit numbers

20 + 6 = 26

30 + 5 = [ ]

20 + 9 = [ ]

40 + 1 = [ ]

[ ] + 8 = 48

[ ] + 6 = 16

50 + [ ] = 53

[ ] + [ ] = 69

Write the missing numbers onto the blank place-value cards.

 ACTION Use place-value cards to make each number.

 THINK Write 'no work' additions for numbers 84 and 97.

29

Creating 2-digit numbers

10 + 7 = ☐

10 + 4 = ☐

20 + 1 = ☐

20 + 5 = ☐

10 + 9 = ☐

20 + 2 = ☐

☐ + 3 = 23

10 + ☐ = 11

Add the pairs of place-value cards together. Write the missing numbers on the blank place-value card.

 ACTION Use place-value cards to make each number.

 THINK I'm thinking of a number. It's got three 10s and five 1s. What is the number?

Identifying odd and even numbers

Count the animal eyes in each tree. Colour all the even numbers red. Write your answer on the trunk.

 Use your blue and red 100-square to help you.

 Children can open one or two eyes. How many children could show 5 eyes altogether?

31

Number sequences

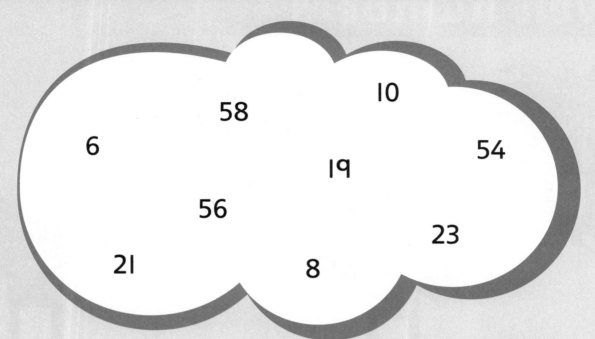

58   10

6   54

19

56

23

21   8

2, 4, ☐, ☐, ☐

13, 15, 17, ☐, ☐, ☐

48, 50, 52, ☐, ☐, ☐

27, 29, 31, ☐, ☐, ☐

Circle the even numbers in the cloud. Write the numbers that come next in the sequences.

 ACTION Use your blue and red 100-square to help you.

 THINK Write your own sequence of five odd numbers.

Complete the patterns

| 12 | 14 | | |

| | | 60 | 70 |

| | | 28 | 30 |

| | 20 | 30 | |

| 10 | 15 | | |

| | | 45 | 50 |

| | 36 | 38 | |

| | 60 | 65 | |

Complete the pattern for each strip.

 ACTION Use a 100-square to help you.

 THINK How far can you count in 5s from 50?

33

Multiplying by 2, 5 and 10

3 lots of 2 =

3 × 2 = ☐

3 lots of 4 =

3 × 4 = ☐

2 lots of 5 =

2 × 5 = ☐

4 × 2 = ☐

5 × 4 = ☐

3 × 3 = ☐

Solve each multiplication. Use the arrays to help you.

 Use cubes to help you.

 Use cubes to make towers. Can you write a number sentence to match?

Doubling

Double $\boxed{5}$ p = $\boxed{10}$ p

Double $\boxed{}$ p = $\boxed{}$ p

Double $\boxed{}$ p = $\boxed{}$ p

Double $\boxed{}$ p = $\boxed{}$ p

Double $\boxed{}$ p = $\boxed{}$ p

Double $\boxed{}$ p = $\boxed{}$ p

Double $\boxed{}$ p = $\boxed{}$ p

Double $\boxed{}$ p = $\boxed{}$ p

Double $\boxed{}$ p = $\boxed{}$ p

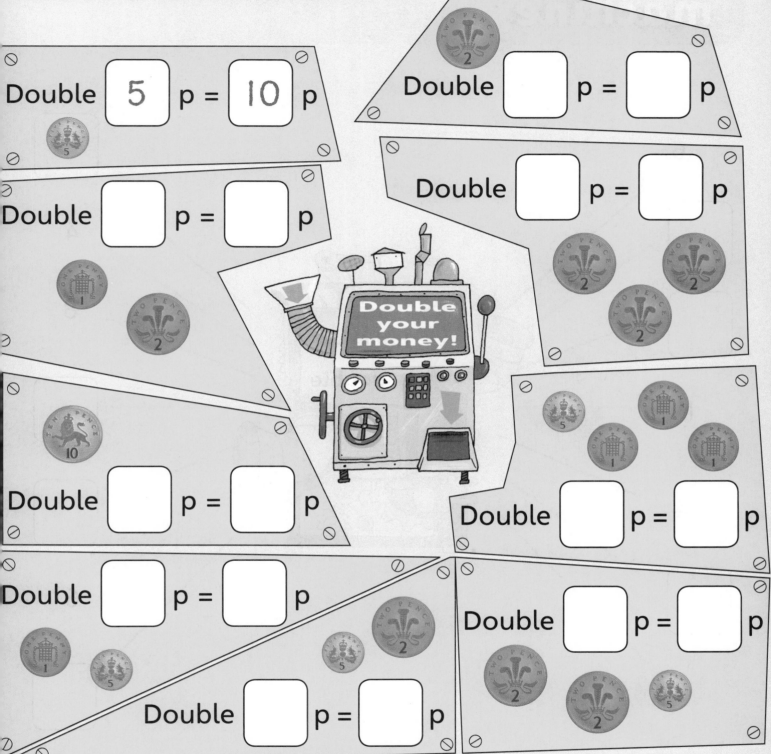

Write the double for each amount put into the machine.

 ACTION Use real coins to help you.

 THINK Which amounts up to 10p can you halve?

Halving and doubling machine

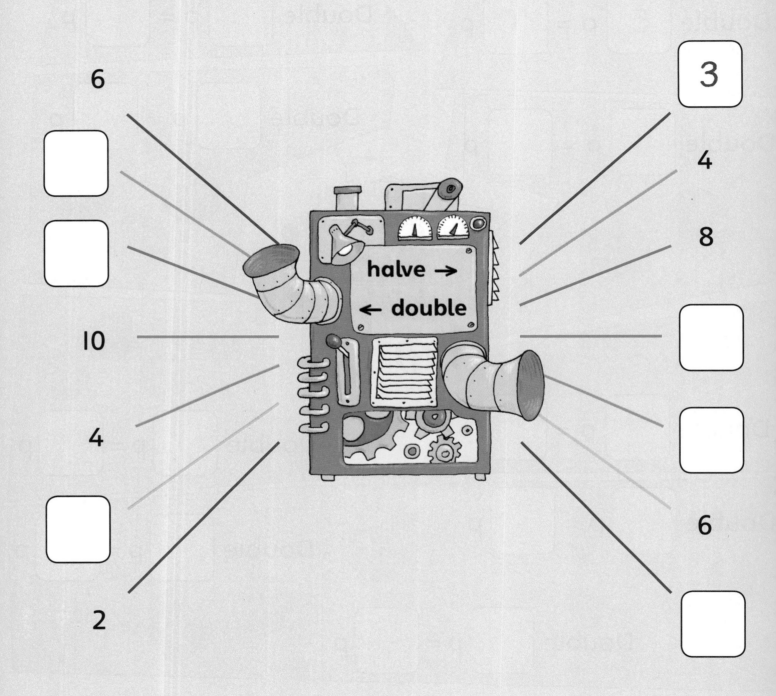

6

3

4

8

10

4

6

2

 Write the numbers that will come out of the halving and doubling machine.

ACTION Use interlocking cubes to help you.

THINK What is half of 9?

Doubles up to 10

Double 5p is [ ] p

2p + 2p = [ ] p

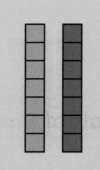

7 + 7 = [ ]

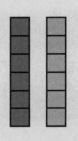

6 + 6 = [ ]

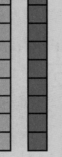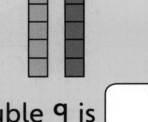

Double 9 is [ ]

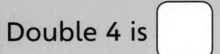

Double 3 is [ ]

Double 4 is [ ]

10p + 10p = [ ] p

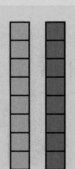

8 + 8 = [ ]

Complete the sentence below each picture.

 ACTION Use interlocking cube towers to do this practically.

 THINK Write I. Double it. Double the answer. Keep going! How far can you go?

Halving

Half of 5 = $\left(2\frac{1}{2},\right)$ $3\frac{1}{2}$,   2

Half of 8 = 4,   3, $4\frac{1}{2}$

Half of 7 = $3\frac{1}{2}$,   3, $7\frac{1}{2}$

Half of 9 = 4, $5\frac{1}{2}$, $4\frac{1}{2}$

Half of 3 = $2\frac{1}{2}$, $1\frac{1}{2}$,   1

Half of 6 = $3\frac{1}{2}$, $2\frac{1}{2}$,   3

Halve the numbers. Circle the right answers.

  Use a fraction strip to help you.

  What do you notice about halving an even number? Is this always true?

O'clock

12 o'clock

7 o'clock

Half past 3

Half past 8

4 o'clock

Quarter past 1

Quarter past 6

Half past 2

Half past 5

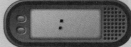

Complete all of the clocks.

Use a clock with moveable hands to help you.

If every clock in a shop shows a different o'clock or half past time, what is the biggest number of clocks there could be?

O'clock

Quarter past 12

12:15

Half past 7

:

Quarter to 9

8:45

Quarter to 11

:

Quarter past 8

:

Quarter to 4

3:45

Quarter past 6

:

Quarter past 2

2:15

Quarter past 1

:

Complete all of the clocks.

 ACTION Use a clock with moveable hands to help you.

 THINK If every clock in a shop shows a different o'clock, half past or quarter past time, what is the biggest number of clocks there could be?

O'clock

Half past 8

7 o'clock

Quarter past 1

1:15

Half past 3

3:30

4 o'clock

Half past 2

2:30

Quarter past 6

Half past 5

12 o'clock

12:00

Complete all of the clocks.

 ACTION Use a clock with moveable hands to help you.

 THINK If every clock in a shop shows a different o'clock time, what is the biggest number of clocks there could be?

41

O'clock

Quarter past 1	Half past 7	Quarter to 9
		 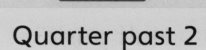

Quarter to 11	Quarter past 8	Quarter past 2

Quarter past 6	Quarter to 4	Quarter past 12
 		 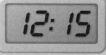

Complete all of the clocks.

 ACTION Use a clock with moveable hands to help you.

 THINK If every clock in a shop shows a different o'clock, quarter to or quarter past time, what is the biggest number of clocks there could be?

Fruit table

Favourite fruit	Number of children
apple	3
banana	8
pear	5
grapes	7
kiwi	4

Fruit	Children
apple	
banana	
pear	
grapes	
kiwi	

 = 1

Complete the pictogram. Which fruit is the most popular? Which fruit is the least popular? How many children prefer grapes?

 ACTION Use counters or interlocking cubes to help you.

THINK How many children prefer fruit that must be peeled? How many children prefer fruit that grows in bunches?

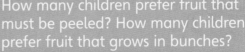

Shapes and patterns

_____

_____

_____

_____

_____

Colour in the shapes to complete the pattern. Next, draw the shapes and colour them in to complete the pattern.

 Use real shapes to make your own repeating patterns.

 Make up your own pattern for a partner to complete.

Addition using bonds to 6, 8 and 9

3 + 5 = ☐

13 + 5 = ☐

23 + 5 = ☐

33 + 5 = ☐

43 + 5 = ☐

6 + 3 = ☐

16 + 3 = ☐

36 + 3 = ☐

56 + 3 = ☐

76 + 3 = ☐

4 + 2 = ☐

24 + 2 = ☐

44 + 2 = ☐

64 + 2 = ☐

94 + 2 = ☐

4 + 4 = ☐

34 + 4 = ☐

54 + 4 = ☐

74 + 4 = ☐

84 + 4 = ☐

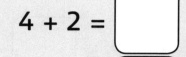

Find the patterns.

Work out the answers for each set of five related questions.

ACTION Use a 100-square or number bonds poster to help you.

THINK If you know that 4 + 3 = 7, what else can you work out really easily?

45

Subtraction using number bonds

5 – 2 =

15 – 2 =

25 – 2 =

35 – 2 =

7 – 4 =

27 – 4 =

57 – 4 =

97 – 4 =

6 – 3 =

26 – 3 =

46 – 3 =

56 – 3 =

8 – 5 =

38 – 5 =

68 – 5 =

88 – 5 =

Find the answers to each set of questions. Use your bonds to do this.

 ACTION Use a 100-square or number bonds posters to help you.

 THINK 7 – 2 = 5
What other subtractions could you work out really easily?

Bonds to 10

5p + ☐ p = 10p

8p + ☐ p = 10p

4p + ☐ p = 10p

2p + ☐ p = 10p

9p + ☐ p = 10p

6p + ☐ p = 10p

3p + ☐ p = 10p

1p + ☐ p = 10p

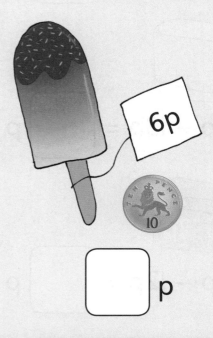

6p

10

☐ p

7p

10

☐ p

Answer the additions. Look at the pictures and write how much change you would get each time.

 ACTION Use counting equipment or a bonds to 10 poster to help you.

 THINK You have a 20p coin. You spend 10p. How much do you have left?

47

Finding change from 20p on a money line

0p   10p   20p

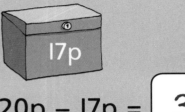

17p

20p – 17p = **3** p

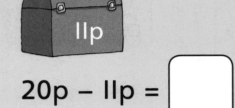

11p

20p – 11p = ☐ p

8p

20p – 8p = ☐ p

15p

20p – 15p = ☐ p

14p

20p – 14p = ☐ p

13p

20p – 13p = ☐ p

18p

20p – 18p = ☐ p

12p

20p – 12p = ☐ p

You have 20p. How much change will you get after buying each item?

 ACTION You can do this practically. Make a line of twenty 1p coins. Subtract each price from these.

 THINK You buy an item for 41p. You pay with a 50p coin. How much change will you get?

48

Finding change from 20p on a money line

0p　　　　　10p　　　　　20p

$20p - 17p =$ **3** p

0p　　　　　10p　　　　　20p

$20p - 12p =$ ☐ p

0p　　　　　10p　　　　　20p

$20p - 9p =$ ☐ p

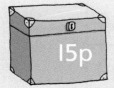

0p　　　　　10p　　　　　20p

$20p - 15p =$ ☐ p

0p　　　　　10p　　　　　20p

$20p - 13p =$ ☐ p

0p　　　　　10p　　　　　20p

$20p - 18p =$ ☐ p

0p　　　　　10p　　　　　20p

$20p - 14p =$ ☐ p

You have 20p. How much change will you get after buying each item?

 ACTION Make a line of twenty 1p coins that you can count along.

 THINK Choose three questions. You did not get your change all in 1ps. How could you have got the change?

Identifying numbers

1	2	3	4	5	6	7	8	9	10
11	12	13	14	15				19	20
21		23	24	25				29	30
			34	35				39	40
41		43		45	46	47	48		
51	52					57	58		
61	62	63		65			68	69	70
71			75				78	79	80
81		83	84	85	86				90
91	92					97	98		100

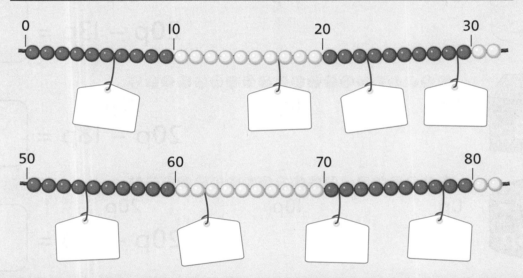

Fill in the missing numbers on the 100-square. Then fill in the tags on the beaded number-lines.

 ACTION Use a 100-square or bead string to help you.

 THINK Using the digits 4, 5 and 7, make four 2-digit numbers. Write them in order, smallest to largest.

2-digit number calculations

Partition these 2-digit numbers into their 10s and 1s. Then combine the 10s and 1s to make a 2-digit number.

 ACTION Use some place-value cards to make each number practically.

 THINK How many different numbers could you make using the 20 card and all of the 1s cards?

51

Adding and subtracting 1

23 + 1 = ▢

42 + 1 = ▢

17 + 1 = ▢

19 + 1 = ▢

49 + 1 = ▢

84 + 1 = ▢

37 − 1 = ▢

22 − 1 = ▢

20 − 1 = ▢

30 − 1 = ▢

40 − 1 = ▢

80 − 1 = ▢

Complete these + 1 and − 1 number sentences.

 ACTION Use a bead string or a 100-square to help you.

 THINK You start with a number and subtract 1. The answer ends in 9. Where might you have started?

54 + 1 = ☐

49 – 1 = ☐

56 – 1 = ☐

87 – 1 = ☐

☐ + 1 = 44

40 – 1 = ☐

39 + 1 = ☐

50 – 1 = ☐

☐ – 1 = 44

☐ – 1 = 93

☐ – 1 = 37

☐ – 1 = 52

Write the missing numbers in each number sentence.

 ACTION Use a bead string or a 100-square to help you.

 THINK 23 + 1 – 1 + 1 + 1 – 1 – 1 =
Work out the answer. What happened?
Write another really long calculation like
this for a partner.

Finding the number above or below

1	2	3	4	5	6	7	8	9	10
11	12	13	14	15	16	17	18	19	20
21	22	23	24	25	26	27	28	29	30
31	32	33	34	35	36	37	38	39	40
41	42	43	44	45	46	47	48	49	50
51	52	53	54	55	56	57	58	59	60
61	62	63	64	65	66	67	68	69	70
71	72	73	74	75	76	77	78	79	80
81	82	83	84	85	86	87	88	89	90
91	92	93	94	95	96	97	98	99	100

88

29

45

11

53

71

13

57

26

17

93

62

Write the numbers that appear directly above or below the number given.

 Use Spider on a 100-square to help you.

THINK Spider starts on 26. She jumps down three spaces. Where does she land? How much has she added?

Adding and subtracting 10

79 – 10 = ☐

63 + 10 = ☐

☐ – 10 = 13

57 – 10 = ☐

☐ + 10 = 55

81 – 10 = ☐

46 + 10 = ☐

☐ – 10 = 33

19 – 10 = ☐

25 + 10 = ☐

☐ – 10 = 99

☐ + 10 = 72

Fill in the missing numbers for each calculation.

ACTION Use Spider on a 100-square to help.

THINK Spider added 10 lots of times to get from 17 to 127. How many times did she add 10?

Freedom when you want it, structure where you choose it.

Abacus is a unique maths toolkit for inspiring a love of maths and ensuring progression for every child. Written by an expert author team, it has been carefully crafted on a robust approach to creating inspired and confident young mathematicians.

Part of the Abacus toolkit, the workbooks provide:

- easy instructions for a teacher to explain to children
- an 'Action' to make the activity more practical
- a 'Think' to provide an extra challenge
- a self-assessment opportunity on every page
- colour to indicate the different maths areas within the programme.

Series Editor: Ruth Merttens   Authors: Jennie Kerwin and Hilda Merttens

Series Editor: Ruth Merttens
Author Team: Jennie Kerwin and Hilda Merttens
Published by Pearson Education Limited, Edinburgh Gate, Harlow, Essex, CM20 2JE.
www.pearsonschools.co.uk

Text © Pearson Education Limited 2014
Page design and layout by room9design
Original illustrations © Pearson Education Limited 2014
Illustrated by Andy Rowland p4, 10, 11, 12, 14, 17–21, 23, 28, 31, 35–36, 47–49; Matt Buckley p6, 22, 39–42, 50; Andrew Painter p47; Volker Beisler p4–5, 7–8, 23–24, 35, 37, 47–49
Cover design by Pearson Education Limited
Cover illustration and Abacus character artwork by Volker Beisler © Pearson Education Limited

First published 2014
19
14
British Library Cataloguing in Publication Data
A catalogue record for this book is available from the British Library

ISBN 9781408278437

Printed in Malaysia (CTP-PJ B)

www.pearsonschools.co.uk | **T** 0845 630 33 33
myorders@pearson.com | **F** 0845 630 77 77

ISBN 978-1-4082-7843-

9 781408 278437